The Art of ideas

Creative Thinking for We

William Duggan and A

Columbia University Press
Publishers Since 1893
New York Chichester West Sussex
cup.columbia.edu
Copyright © 2020 William Duggan, Amy Murphy
All rights reserved

A complete cataloging-in-publication record is available from the Library of Congress.
ISBN 978-0-231-17940-9 (paperback)
ISBN 978-0-231-55142-7 (e-book)
LCCN 2019025479

Columbia University Press books are printed on permanent and durable acid free paper.
This book is printed on paper with recycled content.
Printed in the United States of America

This book is for you:

When you need a new idea.

When you are waiting for inspiration to strike.

When you just don't know what comes next.

The Art of Ideas is about ideas, large and small, in business and life – how they happen, how to spark your own ideas, and what to do while waiting for inspiration to strike.

|||||||||||||||||||||||||||||||||||||||||||||||||||||||||||||||||||||||||||||||||||||

Part I: Idea

A big idea in art	Power & Politics	Business innovation

|||||||||||||||||||||||||||||||||||||||||||||||||||||||||||||||||||||||||||||||||||||

Part II: Method

Rapid appraisal	What Works	Creative Combination

|||||||||||||||||||||||||||||||||||||||||||||||||||||||||||||||||||||||||||||||||||||

Part III: Life

Ideas for Life	Personal strategy	Idea Networking

|||||||||||||||||||||||||||||||||||||||||||||||||||||||||||||||||||||||||||||||||||||

Part I

Idea

A big idea in art.

Chapter 1

Picasso
Self Portrait
1901

The style that
did not make
Picasso famous.

Picasso
Self Portrait
1907

The style that
did make
Picasso famous.

We begin our study of the Art of Ideas with a tale about a big idea in art. Pablo Picasso is the most famous artist of the 20th Century. Amongst famous artists of that time, more people recognize the name Picasso than any other. In 1901, Picasso painted a self-portrait in a style that did not make him famous. In 1907, only six years later, he painted a self-portrait in the style that made him famous.

How did Picasso get the idea to change his style from 1901 to 1907?

The story starts in the middle of the nineteenth century. In England and France they invented the camera, and that threw painters into crisis. They made their living painting portraits and landscapes that people buy and hang on the wall. Now the camera can do that faster and much more cheaply.

But soon after in France, painters invented a new style that saved their day.

Impressionism.

Impressionists broke the scene into little brushstrokes, something a camera could not do. The combination and interplay of different brushstrokes creates the painter's impression of a scene.

From a distance, impressionist paintings look like photographs – they are realistic in color and shape. Up close, they have a rainy day appearance – swirls of color that bring feeling and movement to the scene.

The 1901 Picasso self-portrait is not exactly Impressionism, but from the back of a room, you might think it is a photograph. Now look again at the 1907 Picasso self-portrait. You would have to stand very, very far back to think it is a photograph. This movement away from realism marked the start of Modern Art.

1901   1907

Henri Matisse is credited with the first great painting in Modern Art. It is called Bonheur de Vivre, painted in 1906. Right away you can see that it is not Impressionism. It is not little brushstrokes. It is big patches of color. Matisse called these patches 'volumes of color.' And it is very distorted. You would never think that this painting is a photograph. But it is not completely abstract either. You still recognize trees and goats, people and grass. It is semi-abstract volumes of color... And that was the breakthrough.

At the time, Picasso and Matisse both lived in Paris, the center of art in the western world. Bonheur de Vivre appeared at a Paris exhibition in the spring of 1906. It was an instant sensation. Picasso was twelve years younger than Matisse and very ambitious. He went to the exhibition to study it. Then he went to meet Matisse for the first time.

Nothing happened.

They met again. This second time, Matisse was carrying an African sculpture. This was a time of French colonialism, when African sculpture came to Paris and artists especially collected it.

Upon seeing the African sculpture, Picasso asked Matisse out to dinner. Picasso took the sculpture along to the restaurant. Throughout dinner he moved his mind between Matisse and the sculpture. At the end of dinner he gave the sculpture back to Matisse, and went to his studio to start painting.

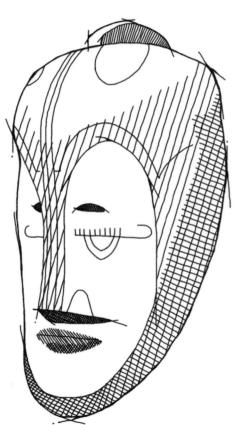

And we know exactly what painting Picasso began to paint that night, because his roommate, Max Jacob, wrote a memoir. And in that book he tells us Picasso began to paint what is still one of the single most famous paintings of Modern Art in the western world:

Desmoiselles d'Avignon

African sculpture

Bonheur de Vivre

Desmoiselles d'Avignon is quite clearly a combination of Matisse's Bonheur de Vivre plus African sculpture. This is how Picasso got his style – combining two pre-existing elements into something new.

Desmoiselles d'Avignon

Most artists know this secret -- that creativity comes from selecting and combining parts of what came before. The poet T.S. Eliot summed it up like this:

Immature poets imitate.

Mature poets steal.

-T.S. Eliot

Sounds easy, right?

Well it's simple in theory, but hard to practice. You follow these steps:

 First you must be able to see things in pieces, to look at a painting or sculpture or anything else as a set of separate elements to put in your memory, each for possible future use in a combination of your own.

 Second, you must clear your mind. You must allow your brain to roam freely amongst the pieces stored on your memory shelves, so that it can select and combine them in a new way.

 Third, you must wait. Once a combination forms, you will experience a flash of insight, the moment where you see your new idea come together in your mind.

 Fourth, you follow through. A strong flash of insight gives you both the idea and the will to see it through. You put your idea into action and make it a reality.

We can see all four steps in Picasso's story.

He saw Matisse's painting and African art in pieces. A relaxing dinner cleared his mind. Selected pieces came together in his brain. He rushed back from dinner with the will to start a new style of painting that very night.

We can find these four steps in case after case of creative success. After all, humans have had new ideas from the beginning of time. That's how we made it out of our caves and came to enjoy the many human wonders that new ideas have yielded over the centuries.

So it's no surprise, we can find these four steps in the new sciences that emerged in the early nineteenth century, as part of the Industrial Revolution.

One of these new sciences was 'strategy': the discipline of forming new ideas for future action. The first classic book of that era was On War by Carl von Clausewitz. This book is still in print, and is recognized as the greatest classic of strategy in the western world.

In this book Clausewitz names our four steps of creative thinking as follows:

1 **Examples from history**

2 **Presence of mind**

3 **Flash of insight**

4 **Resolution**

These four steps will guide us through how creativity happens, and teach you the

Art of ideas.

Power & Politics

Chapter 2

1906
Mohandas Gandhi

1937
Mahatma Gandhi

The time is the early 1900s. The place is South Africa.
The country is still part of the British Empire, although Dutch settlers fight for and win local control in half the country.

South Africa

The Dutch call themselves Afrikaners, and they aim to put in place racial laws that later become known as "apartheid." There are Indian immigrants in the country too, and they form a South African Indian Congress to oppose these racial laws. Their method is lawful and polite: they put together delegations of prominent Indians to ask the British authorities to grant them full and equal rights. They copy this method and name from the Indian National Congress. India is also part of the British Empire, and Indians are second-class citizens in their own country.

In 1906, the South African Indians send the secretary of their organization to London to lobby the British authorities directly. He is thirty-seven years old, small, quiet, and shy. He wears a proper English lawyer suit.

He was born in India. He failed as a lawyer there, moved to South Africa, and failed as a lawyer there too. The South African Indians pay him just enough to live on.

His name is Mohandas Gandhi.

When he arrives in London, he finds the country in an uproar over the tactics of Emmeline Pankhurst, the English suffragette. For years English women had used the same method as the Indians in South Africa and India: polite delegations to ask the authorities for their rights. Then Pankhurst broke away to form a new organization with a different idea that she took directly from the British labor movement...

Before Emmeline Pankhurst...

After Emmeline Pankhurst...

You get arrested. You go to jail in droves. The labor movement had such success with these tactics in Britain that in 1906 it formed its own Labour Party, with twenty-nine Members of Parliament elected. Pankhurst started to use the same tactics, and she started to win, as British officials one by one declared their support for women's suffrage, including Winston Churchill.

Illegal marches

Demonstrations

Parades

Picketing

Gandhi sees the light. It changes his life. When he gets back to South Africa, he writes in his local Indian newspaper:

WHEN WOMEN ARE MANLY, WILL MEN BE EFFEMINATE? A FEW DAYS AGO A PROCESSION OF EIGHT HUNDRED WOMEN MARCHED TO THE HOUSES OF PARLIAMENT. WHEN THE POLICE STOPPED THE CROWD, SOME BRAVE WOMEN TRIED TO FORCE THEIR WAY INTO THE HOUSE. . . . THE MAGISTRATE SENTENCED THEM . . . AND EACH ONE OF THEM, INSTEAD OF PAYING UP THE PITTANCE OF A FINE, HAS COURTED IMPRISONMENT. . . . WE BELIEVE THAT THESE WOMEN HAVE BEHAVED IN A MANLY WAY.
NOW LET US LOOK AT OUR OWN HOUSE. . . . WILL INDIANS GO TO GAOL . . . ? . . . HENCE WE ASK: WILL INDIAN MEN BE EFFEMINATE? OR WILL THEY EMULATE THE MANLINESS SHOWN BY THE ENGLISH WOMEN AND WAKE UP?
BRAVE WOMEN OF BRITAIN. . . . ALL OF THEM GO TO GAOL INSTEAD OF PAYING FINES. . . . WE HAVE TO FOLLOW THE EXAMPLE OF THE WOMEN REFERRED TO ABOVE. WE EARNESTLY REQUEST ALL OUR READERS TO HAVE THIS ARTICLE IMPRINTED ON THEIR MINDS.
WOMEN IN ENGLAND HAVE SURPASSED ALL EXPECTATIONS. . . . INDIANS HAVE TO FIGHT WITH THE SAME SPIRIT.

An example from history leads Gandhi to change his strategy. He brings Pankhurst's passive resistance back to the South African Indian Congress.

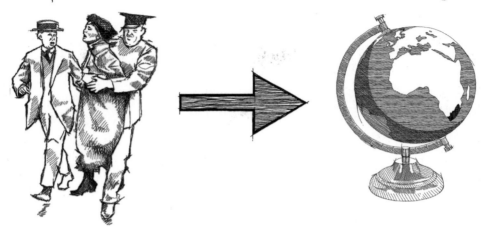

After ten years of struggle in South Africa, Gandhi returns to India to take the same idea to the Indian National Congress. He becomes its leader in 1924. Of course his flash of insight in London was not the whole story: there were years of further refinement, ups and downs and twists and turns. But once again, there would not even be a story if not for his flash of insight. Before his big idea, you would not have picked him out of a crowd. After, he became the most famous person on earth.

And his methods became a model—an example from history all its own—for other leaders and movements in their own struggles, most famously Martin Luther King and American civil rights.

Gandhi's presence of mind and flash of insight gave him the new goal for South African Indians to apply the techniques of nonviolent civil disobedience from Emmeline Pankhurst's example from history. But how to do that, exactly?

Gandhi wisely saw that the two situations were different enough that he needed more elements to combine. For example, the English women were a homogeneous group: middle class, educated, English speakers, almost all of the same religion, and of course, all women. Indians in South Africa were rich and poor, Hindu and Muslim and Christian, literate and illiterate, male and female, merchants and laborers. They spoke various Indian languages, and the Hindus were further divided by caste, with Untouchables at the very bottom.

How would Gandhi bring them together?

Again, the solution came from presence of mind. Instead of doing exactly what Pankhurst did, Gandhi opened his mind and saw another example from history to add. This one came from Russia.

Leo Tolstoy was a Russian noble. After completing his great novels, Tolstoy turned his family estate into a classless society. His followers set up Tolstoyan communes to follow his principles of perfect equality among all people, where all could live and work together. So Gandhi set one up in South Africa. He called it, "Tolstoy Farm." Gandhi moved there to live. There he gave up his lawyer suits for simple Indian clothes, again like Tolstoy, who on his estate dressed like a Russian peasant.

Tolstoy

Gandhi

When Gandhi moved back to India, he set up the same thing there but gave it an Indian name: "ashram," which Indians recognized as the site where a holy man lives and gives instruction to others.

At that point Gandhi started dressing even more simply, in bolts of white cloth like a Hindu holy man—yet another example from history that all Indians knew quite well.

Tolstoy Farm

Women's Suffrage + **Tolstoy** + **Hindu Holy Man** = **Mahatma Gandhi**

Presence of mind means that all the elements of your idea are open to alteration, all the time. You ask yourself every morning: Is there something I need to add, subtract, or change?

The answer is probably no. But if you don't ask, you'll miss that rare time when the answer is yes. Changing your idea every day is bad—you'll never get anywhere. But staying open every day to changing your idea—that's essential to presence of mind.

In 1906, when Gandhi went to London to lobby British authorities, he had the presence of mind to notice Emmeline Pankhurst's methods and change course immediately. Similarly, Gandhi benefited from the presence of mind of others.

In 1915, after twenty years in South Africa, Gandhi returned to India. At that point, he was a newcomer to the independence movement there. For those same twenty years, a whole generation of leaders had toiled away in India. They were "experts" in the Indian independence movement.

But rather than clinging to their previous ideas, many of them switched to Gandhi's new idea—including his two greatest allies, Jawaharlal Nehru and Sardar Patel, who became independent India's first prime minister and deputy prime minister. They had the presence of mind, and the humility, to accept someone else's idea.

Mohandas Gandhi   **Mahatma Gandhi**

Business innovation

Chapter 3

It's 1997, and Reed Hastings has just sold a successful software company, founded ten years before when he was just out of college. He's living in San Jose, California, and goes to the video store to return the movie Apollo 13. It's woefully late, so he pays a $40 late fee. He's dismayed and embarrassed.

"How will he tell his wife? Hmm... does he have to tell her? Oh, great! Now I'm thinking about lying to my wife about a late fee and the sanctity of my marriage..."

He drives from the video store to his gym club. On the way, something strikes him:

"Whoa! Video stores could operate like a gym, with a flat membership fee. I wonder why nobody's done that before?"

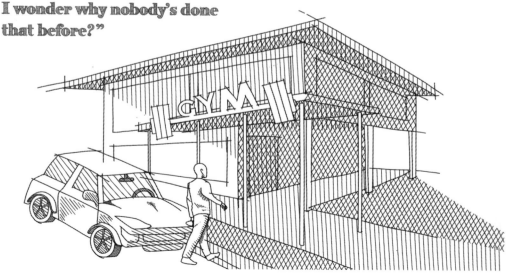

Two thoughts come together to form a new idea: video stores and gym clubs. At the time, American video stores were big box stores filled with racks of videocassettes that customers browsed through to rent and pay for one at a time. Blockbuster was the largest chain in the country. Meanwhile, gym clubs were open workout areas with lots of machines that members used freely.

Blockbuster + GYM

Hastings pairs the whole Blockbuster operation, minus the payment system, with the membership system at gym clubs. This was the premise of Netflix, unlimited movie rentals for one flat fee.

But that's not all. To make this vision a reality he pulls in additional inspiration from other fields as well.

Amazon is two years old at the time, and has already pioneered many of the features of e-commerce that we now take for granted, including safe payment with credit cards. Hastings takes many of these e-commerce features from Amazon, including the very basic concepts of online purchase and mail delivery. Yet Hastings hits a snag: video-cassettes are bulky and too expensive to mail.

A friend tells Reed Hastings about a new technology for movies that just reached the American market from Japan: the digital video disc, or DVD. It's far lighter and smaller than a Blockbuster videocassette. That makes it much easier to mail.

> **"I ran down to Tower Records and bought a bunch and mailed them to myself and then I waited... And I opened them up. And they were fine. And I thought,... Oh my God. This is gonna work!"**
>
> **— Reed Hastings**

It was the combination of all these elements that launched Netflix. Hastings's idea had little to do with his own past experience or software expertise. Thousands of people knew enough about Blockbuster, Amazon, gym clubs and DVDs to have the same idea. And while his knowledge of software probably helped him implement this idea, the idea itself included no actual software innovations.

In this way, the Art of Ideas transcends your own experience and expertise. Instead you look outside yourself. If Hastings had limited his thinking to his own head he never would have had his big idea. This means that your own experience and expertise can be a barrier to innovation.

Blockbuster

✝ **GYM**

✝ **Amazon**

✝ **DVD Video**

= **Netflix**

Once an idea has formed and taken shape, it becomes an element for others to use in new ideas. This was the case for Netflix, when a business school student, Katrina Lake, was looking to make curated fashion more accessible.

Lake was an avid cook and part of a Community Supported Agriculture (CSA) that delivered a box of fresh, seasonal fruits and vegetables to her Cambridge apartment. She frequently received fashion advice from her sister who knew her desired style and worked in the New York fashion industry. These elements combined with Netflix's e-commerce model to create curated fashion delivery - a.k.a, Stitch Fix.

For a small fee, customers receive shipments of clothing based on their size, tastes, and information culled from social media accounts. Customers pay for the items they want to keep, and return what they don't want.

Lake's idea was so successful that she became the youngest female founder to take a company public. Stitch Fix is a $2 Billion company today.

Regardless of the field - art, politics, business, fashion, etc. - the rules of creativity are the same. Ideas are combinations of pre-existing elements. These examples from history require presence of mind to spark this combination, and then resolution to action to see it through. In the next chapter we will show you a formal method to generate ideas based on how ideas happen. It mirrors what happens in your brain to produce the same kind of flashes of insight that give Picasso, Gandhi, Hastings and Lake their big ideas.

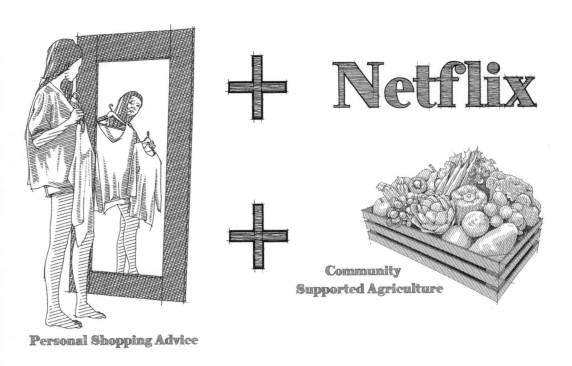

Personal Shopping Advice + Netflix + Community Supported Agriculture

= Stitch Fix

Part II

Method

Rapid appraisal

Chapter 4

You have seen how ideas come together in the human mind in a natural way, at their own pace, in their own time. Of course that's best, but sometimes, you can't wait. You need an innovation sooner rather than later, in your work or your personal life. Here we offer a formal method to help. It matches the four steps of creative thinking as much as possible in a deliberate and organized way. We have used this method at Columbia Business School and PwC's Strategy& to help people and companies around the world create new ideas. Here are the steps.

First, you need a problem to solve. And then ask yourself: does it need a creative solution? Most of the time the answer is no. If you can solve the problem by research into that field or industry, or by asking a subject matter expert, then you don't need a new idea. You just need time to uncover an answer that already exists.

On the other hand, if you have a problem that no one has solved before, not even experts in the field, then you have a creative problem that calls for a creative solution. You need a new idea. The formal method for finding one follows this sequence:

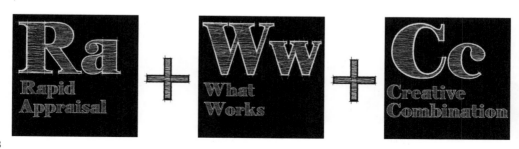

We start with Rapid Appraisal. It means simply that – appraise your problem rapidly to grasp its many facets. Rapid here means pragmatic.

You won't have time to understand every single thing there is to know about the problem, but you need to know enough to break the problem down into its most critical elements. That gives you the pieces of the puzzle. Solve the pieces, you solve the puzzle.

How do I start?

First, write down the problem. State it in a terse, simple way. If possible, pare it down to one sentence that describes the problem plainly. It helps to put the problem in the form of a question, so that it is clear what you are looking to answer.

Sample problems:

What career should I pursue?

How do we differentiate an undifferentiated product?

How do we overcome negative stigmas?

How do we extend our brand?

...?

Note that each of the sample problems gets straight to the point. Shorter is better. Avoid developing a long-winded paragraph that is full of excessive details. When you try to capture too much information, the most meaningful parts get lost.

As the philosopher Blaise Pascal explained:

"I only made this longer because I did not have time to make it shorter."

Once you have clearly laid out your problem, the next step is to gather information about it. The best way to do this is by interviewing stakeholders and experts who are familiar with the problem.

Why conduct interviews?

Interviews help you to identify the long list of issues that make up your problem. Interviews also help to broaden your perspective on the problem through different viewpoints.

How do you structure a good interview?

A good interview is a series of open-ended questions that you think through beforehand and that can each be answered in a statement or two. Avoid yes/no questions.

For example?

Start with: Why is this a problem? Continue to follow up with "Why is that" or "What other issues are preventing this problem from being solved?" Continue to ask your interviewee "why?" until you understand the many issues that make up your problem.

Why? ... Why? ... Why? ...

During the interviews, keep an open mind and listen to your interviewee. It is important to learn their perspective on the issues to broaden your understanding of the problem. Remember, you are not looking to solve the problem during the interview. You are trying to understand it. And take notes. A good tactic is to split your interview notes into sections. Once the interview is complete, force yourself to write the key takeaway for each of these sections. Often, the takeaways are the long-list of issues to your problem. This list is all of the reasons that your problem cannot be solved. No reason is too small or insignificant when creating a long list. The more thorough your interviews and research of the problem, the more robust and significant your long list of issues will be.

Sample Interview Notes:

Problem: How do we differentiate an undifferentiated product?

Q1: Why is your product undifferentiated?
We are one of ten plus players in this market, and all have similar products. The efficacy of our product is technically better, but we are unable to promote this due to federal regulations.

➡️ **Inability to promote superior efficacy of product**

Q2: How do the federal regulations prevent you from promoting superior efficacy?

Q3: Is your product different from competition in any other ways?

Q4: In what ways is your product the same as competition?

Once you have completed interviews and conducted research on your problem, you need to condense the long list of issues into 2-7 key elements of your problem.

How do you identify the key elements?

First, take your long list of the many issues you uncovered, then identify which ones are most critical and which ones can be grouped together. If your problem can be solved without solving for one particular issue, then that issue isn't critical. The remaining issues, those that need to be solved, are the key elements of your problem.

Why 2-7 key elements?

Ideally, your problem will decompose into 2 - 7 elements. If you only have one element, then that element is your problem and you need to further break it down. If you have more than seven elements, it is too many for a human mind to juggle at once.

If you have more than seven elements, we suggest taking the biggest of these elements and making it the problem you are trying to solve. Then break that problem down into its key elements. You will need to first solve this piece of the problem, before addressing the original, larger problem.

For example?

Let's say that we are executives of a low cost, high volume, self-assembled furniture store chain and we are faced with a problem: many customers buy our funiture in their young, unmarried years, but move on to other stores when they get married or rise to higher income jobs. After several iterations and discussions, we arrive at the problem "How do we retain customers when they transition from young adult to working professional?"

We conduct interviews with customers (various ages, demographics), employees (varying tenure, departments, demographics) and find a long list of issues.

- Furniture is seen as inexpensive, temporary
- Furniture is not associated with "successful / high-end"
- Furniture is difficult to move once assembled
- Consumers tend to only shop at our store at the time they move
- Shopping takes time – requires selecting, transporting and assembling
- Working professionals don't have a lot of time
- Furniture can be frustrating to assemble
- Purchasing assembly & shipping puts pricing at same level as other brands
- Online order selection is limited, young professionals tend to order online
- Retail stores aren't always convenient to get to (distance, traffic, etc.)
- Store has limited touch points with consumers (only when in the store)
- Outside small group of loyalists, limited brand zealots...

We then start to condense this list into buckets and elevate the issues which need to be solved in order to solve our problem.

Initial list of elements:
- Brand has a stigma: inexpensive / young / short-term
- Lack strong consumer engagement
- Products require effort/time, something young professionals don't have

Once you have an initial list of elements, you should work to rephrase these elements to be agnostic of industry and company context. If your elements are written so that they are laser-focused on one industry it limits your mindset. Writing elements agnostic of industry encourages you to think broadly and drives cross-industry/era/geographic inspiration.

Rapid appraisal of the problem:

Problem: How do we retain customers as they transition from young adult to working professional?

Key Elements:
- **Brand has a distinct stigma**
- **Limited consumer engagement**
- **Product requires more effort; customers have less time**

 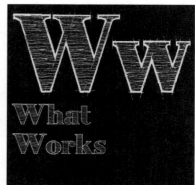

What Works

Chapter 5

Now you search.

Once you have clearly defined the problem and its key elements, you are ready for the next step – finding examples of anybody, anywhere, anytime that has solved any aspect of that element before. These examples are called precedents and showcase what has worked before.

Looking through history includes what people often think of as "current". But the reality is we have no idea what is "current" -- CNN reports what happened "moments ago", that is, in the past. Yesterday is history, last month is history, last century is history.

Are precedents the same thing as best practices?

Frequently companies look for best practices to adopt or benchmark against. Best practices are typically different from precedents. Best practices are the equivalent of what you would like to do. Let's say you are a consumer-packaged goods company trying to generate better consumer insights. You might look to see what your competitors are doing to generate consumer insights and mirror the "best practices" you find. This is focused on matching industry standard or best-in-class. It is not about innovating in the field of consumer insights.

For innovation, you need ideas and inspiration beyond what is happening today, in your immediate field. This requires precedents from wider afield: partial solutions to your problem that help inspire new thinking.

Best Practice:

— An exact match from the same industry

— Not a novel solution

Precedent:

— Can come from any industry or sector

— An example from history that worked

— Partial match- that solves an element of the problem

— Used as inspiration for a novel combination

How do you start searching for precedents?

Precedents exist anywhere there is a story about an accomplishment that details how it was done. Steve Jobs got inspiration for the Apple genius bar from hotel concierge services. Inspiration for Henry Ford's assembly line came from a slaughterhouse.

Your goal: to seek inspiration from anywhere around the world and back through time.

First, remove any judgments about what the solution to the problem could be. Focus on one element at a time in a way that is agnostic about the particular field. Then ask: How has this piece of the puzzle been solved before?

You can write the element as a list of sub-questions to help drive your thinking.

Example element:
Lacking consumer engagement

— **Who has engaged consumers in a non-traditional way?**

— **Who has developed good rapport with their customers?**

— **Who has created interactive exchanges?**

— **When and where has the relationship endured?**

— **...?**

Each of the questions you develop inspires you to think about different angles on the element of consumer engagement. Here are some possible precedents for this element:

Serial Podcast

The podcast Serial engaged consumers in a non-traditional way – it provided listeners a front row seat as information is uncovered.

Zappos

Zappos customer service developed good rapport with customers through free shipping / free returns and developed highly interactive product content (videos, photos, multi-dimensional search attributes).

The 2014 ALS Ice bucket challenge for Lou Gehrig's disease became an engaging, viral exchange amongst people across the world (it made sharing on social media integral to the activity).

Lego + Nasa

NASA and Lego have had an ongoing partnership since 2010 to drive education, encourage creative talent, and push more children into STEM careers by developing fun, creative ways to engage children like "design and build" events.

Your immediate memory can yield some precedents, but the most important search tool is something with lots more examples stored: the internet. Filter each of your questions as a search term. Go through the search hits to look for any examples of how this has been solved before.

As you search the internet, also be sure to:
- Search via images or videos in addition to web pages
- Replace parts of your question with synonyms to get more varied results
- Add key words like example, how, success, award

Once you have exhausted internet search – begin crowd sourcing. Ask friends, colleagues, or relatives the search questions. But don't tell them what the initial problem is. Limit your discussion about the problem to an element and its search questions. This enables people to think as broadly as possible, without constraints.

The next place to look is newspapers, articles, and everyday experience. Don't feel forced to find answers. Take a break, go for a walk, and allow your mind to wander. Breaks are an important part of the method, they give your mind time to wander freely through what you found so far. When you find a precedent that addresses an element – jot it down. Capture the key points:

-Background   -Evidence of success
-Insights   -Applicability

Let's go back to our furniture problem. Here is an example of a successful search for one of its key elements:

Element: Brand has a distinct stigma
Example search question: Who has reversed a stigma?
Precedent: Intermarché – inglorious fruits and vegetables

Background

- Intermarché, a French grocery chain, launched a food waste reduction campaign called "Inglorious Fruits & Vegetables"
- Intermarché negotiated with farmers to purchase deformed produce that didn't meet typical grocery store aesthetic standards and would have been discarded
- Intermarché sold the deformed fruits and vegetables at a 30% discount

Insights

- Accentuate faults: Intermarché did not try to pass the produce off as "normal", instead they characterized and exaggerated the abnormal traits (e.g., the disfigured eggplant, the failed lemon)
- Elevate advantages: Intermarche highlighted that these foods taste just as good as "normal" produce by sampling and selling smoothies and soups made from deformed produce
- Story-telling: each fruit and vegetable had a name and background, humanizing the produce and making it more personable and appealing

THE FAILED LEMON

FROM THE CREATOR OF THE LEMON.

THE RIDICULOUS POTATO

ELECTED MISS MASHED POTATO 2014.

A GROTESQUE APPLE

A DAY KEEPS THE DOCTOR AWAY AS WELL.

Intermarché
Inglorious
fruits & vegetables

Source: Intermarché Inglorious Fruits & Vegetables Campaign

Evidence of success

- In one month, Intermarché sold 1.2 tons per store of inglorious fruits and vegetables (1,800 stores, saving 2,160 tons of food waste)
- Each store saw an ~24% increase in traffic as a result of the campaign

Applicability

- How could the chain furniture store flip the conversation?
- How could the chain furniture store leverage story-telling and campaigns to change the impression of its products?

After you have gathered the key information for each precedent, you will have a library of precedent profiles. Filter these down and place the most relevant and applicable ones into a grid. We call this grid an insight matrix. It gathers into one place your problem, its most important elements, and the precedents that address those elements.

Insight Matrix

How do we retain customers as they transition from young adult to working professional?

Brand has a distinct stigma	Intermarché Lifeproof
Limited consumer engagement	Serial Podcast Zappos  Lego + Nasa
Product requires more effort; customers have less time	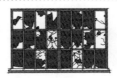 Uber

When do you stop the search?

The best answer is: When you get an idea! That is, some subset of the precedents comes together in your mind. But if that doesn't happen -- yet -- you stop your search when you run out of time, or precedents get harder and harder to find. Twenty to forty precedents is a good target for most situations. At that point you're ready for the next step of the method.

 **Ra**
Rapid
Appraisal

 +

 **Ww**
What
Works

 +

 **Cc**
Creative
Combination

Creative Combination

Chapter 6

Once you have a full insight matrix -- with problem, elements and precedents, we move to our third step of the method: creative combination. This is when the pieces of your new idea finally come together in your mind. Because this step differs so much from other creative methods you might know or have tried before, first we give you a way to practice, before trying it on your own idea. This practice takes the form of a game. You can play it alone or with a group. The game takes about an hour to do. By the end, you will feel creative, because you see how creativity works and know that you can do it. Then you will be ready to apply creative combination to your own problems.

cre·a·tive:
having the
power to
create

Lots of people think they're not creative because they think 'creative' means 'artistic.' They can't dance, they can't sing, they can't draw. But 'creative' actually means 'having the power to create' -- and you can do that in any field, not just the arts. This game gives you practice in creating an 'innovation,' which means 'something new and useful.' You see that you can be creative by learning how creativity works, and by doing it yourself.

in·no·va·tion:
something
new and useful

To start the game, open the book to the previous page and lay it flat on a table. Stand a few steps away and throw a coin three times so that it lands on three different objects, or you can close your eyes and touch a finger to three pictures at random. Write down the three objects on a sheet of paper. If you're in a group, use flip chart paper so everyone can see.

Now here is your task: put these three objects together to make something new and useful -- that is, an innovation.

But wait. Remember that you know the secret to innovation. You don't just push the three together. If you got an egg, a camel, and a torch and you smoosh them together you get a broken egg, and a burned camel. That's not right.

From our earlier steps of rapid appraisal and what works, we know what to do. We aren't going to imitate the camel, we are going to steal from the camel. We don't want the whole camel, we want a part of the camel. Break each object down into its elements. What can I steal from a camel? An egg? A torch? Write down the elements of each object and then see what combinations these could create.

Here is an example we did ourselves. We randomly chose three objects,

and then broke them down as follows...

What Works?

> webbed feet for swimming

> buoyant body shape

> wings for flying

> natural bunches

> disposable skin

> easy to open

> slip-on

> cheap

> waterproof

Now remove the objects and let your mind wander instead among the elements:

webbed feet

buoyant body shape

wings for flying

natural bunches

disposable skin

easy to open

slip-on

cheap

waterproof

Remember, you're not combining the objects. You're making some combination of the elements. Stare at the elements for a while. If you get stuck, get up, grab a coffee, go for a walk. After awhile you will start to see things. Combinations of elements that make something real.

What did we see?

buoyant body shape

cheap

slip-on

disposable skin

natural bunches

easy to open

waterproof

What is it?

Disposable, inflatable pillows for travel, in multi-packs.

We combined seven things: buoyant body shape, cheap, slip-on, easy to open, disposable skin, waterproof and natural bunches. We're not saying it's a great idea, but this is how we came up with it. We combined seven elements.

It's important to note the elements you combined. That way when you explain your idea to others, they can see how you came up with it. This is important for real creative ideas, it helps others to make the connection in their own minds and thus "see" the idea.

Now remember this is a game. You're not trying to engineer a real product. It's amazing the crazy inventions people come up with. The goal is to have fun and exercise your mind. The point of this game is to show people who think they aren't creative, just how creative they can be. And how creativity means combining what has worked before.

Last but not least, sketch your new creation and give it a name.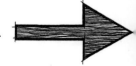

Zzz·Mobile

Now that you have practiced creative combination as a game, let's go back to our real example, the furniture problem. We gather the most relevant and important precedents and put them into an insight matrix:

How do we retain customers as they transition from young adult to working professional?

Brand has a distinct stigma	Intermarché	Lifeproof
Limited consumer engagement	Serial Podcast Zappos	Lego + Nasa
Product requires more effort; customers have less time	 	Uber

What combinations could these precedents make?

For each precedent, consider "what works". And then start combining the items that work. For example, could Serial's ability to make the consumer a part of the process combine with Intermarche's ability to showcase the truth (food tastes good, regardless of its appearance)? Could Zappos's search functionality combine with Uber's on-demand model?

As you combine precedents you generate ideas. For each idea, write down:

- what is the idea   - how does it address the problem
- how does it work   - what are the next steps to put this into action

If you are in a group and looking to innovate, lead a discussion around the precedents - this is different from brainstorming where you throw out solutions. Here you state precedents that might serve as a piece of a solution. The Art of Ideas is based on the parts of your problem and inspiration that addresses each one. It is combinations of what has worked before.

What if you don't come up with any ideas?

In our experience, if you go through the steps of breaking down the problem into elements, thoroughly searching for precedents, and then working to combine these precedents through an insight matrix - you will come up with at least one idea. The process itself unlocks new ways of thinking about your problem and draws on diverse input into potential solutions. But still, it is possible that the idea you come up with is just not sound enough to solve the problem. After all, we cannot solve every problem on earth. If we could, we would live in a paradise, not the world as we know it. Even so, we recommend going back to the search or breaking the problem down even further. Take one element as your problem and work to develop ideas that solve that one piece of the problem. Then, go back and do the same for your other elements. Look for more inspiration to your problem.

Don't forget to stop and take a break, to let your mind wander away from what you have found.

Inspiration usually happens when you are relaxed and at ease. We call this state "presence of mind". The two biggest obstacles to presence of mind are excessive focus and negative emotions. Excessive focus means you can't let go of your current understanding of the problem, your goals, your timeline, options you've already listed, and so on. You must free your mind of all that, to let your brain make new connections. And negative emotions of all kinds – anger, frustration, worry, fear – flood the brain with the hormone cortisol, which blocks recall of what you have stored in memory. You literally cannot think creatively. So when you are stuck, take the time to step away and relax.

When your mind is clear it will look to combine what is on its memory shelves and then... 'aha!" you will have a flash of insight - a combination of examples from history that form an idea. It may not be one big "Eureka!" moment -- instead it may be a series of smaller ones that you hardly feel as discrete cognitive events. Regardless, the mental mechanism is the same for large and small epiphanies - it is a feeling of excitement as the idea forms.

Remember the Netflix story?

Reed Hastings had an initial spark of inspiration, then a combination of further pieces made this idea come to life.

The initial 'aha!' moment brought two elements together: Blockbuster video rental plus gym membership. That made a flat-rate movie subscription service like gym memberships, to watch as much or as little as you want, with no late fees.

To make this idea a reality, it required two more sources of inspiration:
- Amazon's internet retail model
- Lightweight DVD technology for easy mailing

Blockbuster **GYM** **Amazon** **DVD Video**

And then, Reed Hastings had to see it through - he had the resolution to act on the idea. At the beginning of the book we introduced the four key concepts that Hastings clearly followed:

1 Examples from history

2 Presence of mind

3 Flash of insight

4 Resolution

This chapter gives you a method to get to #3 via #1 and #2. And we saw for Hastings and Gandhi especially that #4 - Resolution - included a repeat of steps #1-3 to solve smaller problems along the way.

First you must be able to see things in pieces, as a set of elements to put in your memory, for possible future use in a combination of your own.

 Second, you must clear your mind. You must allow your brain to roam freely amongst the pieces stored in your memory shelves, so that it can select and combine them in a new way.

 Third, you must wait. Once a combination forms, you will experience a flash of insight, the moment where you see your new idea come together.

 Fourth, you follow through. A strong flash of insight gives you both the idea and the will to see it through. You put your idea into action and make it a reality.

Resolution, number four, is the difference between a great innovation and a lost idea. The last step in Creative Combination and The Art of Ideas is to put the work in to enable your idea to take flight and become a reality. Don't forget to repeat steps 1-3 as needed to solve problems you encounter during Resolution.

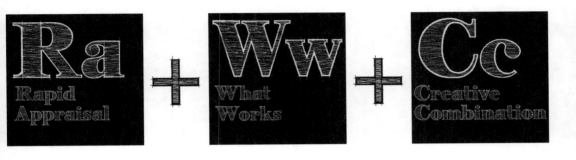

Ra — Rapid Appraisal + Ww — What Works + Cc — Creative Combination

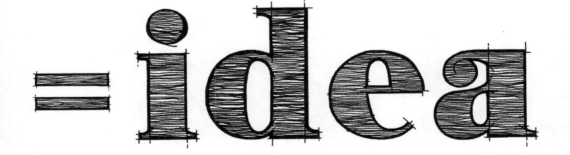

= idea

Part IIII

Life

Ideas for Life

Chapter 7

Some new ideas lead to major changes in how the world works, but the majority of them just change the world of one person. Behind the scenes, lost to history, are millions of new and useful ideas that solve individual problems of life or work. A painful familial or romantic relationship might call for a new and useful idea to heal it, or a project might get bogged down at work and needs a new idea to save it. These personal creative ideas, for work or life, are just as important for advancing human achievement and the quality of our lives as great innovations like electric light or the personal computer. And they happen in your brain in exactly the same way too.

While you cannot will an epiphany to happen, you can improve your ability to be creative and your likelihood of having these "aha" moments. Remember, the epiphany itself is just #3 of the four steps of the Art of Ideas:

The Art of ideas

1 **Examples from history**
2 **Presence of mind**
3 **Flash of insight**
4 **Resolution**

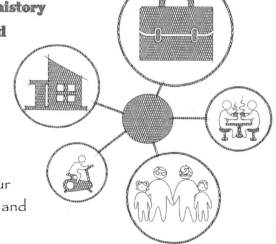

We often separate work problems from personal problems, but in reality your personal life includes your work life. In a typical month, you spend more of your waking time working than with your family and friends or in down time alone.

And your thoughts about your work include its personal side: for example, how to fulfill your interests and passions at your current job, whether to look for a different job, how to deal with difficult people at work, or how much time and thought to devote to work versus the other parts of your life. And new ideas in your work are personal too: innovation is always a risk, and takes personal commitment on the part of the innovator. So having new ideas at work, and deciding whether or not to commit to them, is an integral part of your personal life.

The goal of Part III of this book is to help you improve your ability to create new and useful ideas for changing something about your life.

New ideas are not the only way to change your life: for example, you can learn a new language or move to a new country, make new friends or find a new job. But when taking any of these steps, you run into a problem, you might need a creative idea to solve it. That's when you need the Art of Ideas.

The Art of Ideas is a general skill - it applies to the generation of any new idea. Improving your ability to create new and useful ideas helps you at work, home, school and life. Even a small improvement in this ability could yield tremendous impact. You can learn the right mental steps to prepare your brain for a flash of insight, and you can learn how to follow through after it happens.

Examples from history

We saw that the first step of the Art of Ideas is: Examples from history. Your mind searches the content in its memory and looks to combine elements to generate a new idea. Here is how Gwen Stefani, the singer, songwriter, fashion designer, dancer, producer and actor describes it:

People might think you can turn creativity on and off, but it's not like that. It just kind of comes out: a mash-up of all these things you collect in your mind. You never know when it's going to happen, but when it does, it's like magic. It's just that easy, and it's just that hard.

- Gwen Stefani

So your first step is to fill your memory shelves -- the "things you collect in your mind." From the moment you are born, your brain takes in these examples and stores them in your memory for possible use in the future. This is how you learned to walk, talk, eat, dress, and to do most of what you know how to do: by learning what other people did, and then doing it yourself. As you grow older and keep on learning, you have more and more examples to draw from, and these become the building blocks for your own ideas of what to do yourself in the future.

You add to your memory shelves the more you read, experience, explore and absorb examples. The discipline of seeing and considering what is happening around you lays the ground work for generating ideas. As with any habit, the more you do it, the easier it gets. You can practice gathering examples when reading newspapers or magazines. Look for articles that explain how someone achieved something, and when you find one, try to work through exactly what that person did to succeed. It doesn't matter if they're working in an area that you don't know much about. Some of the best ideas take elements from far and wide.

You can also practice at meetings or at parties, or whenever you meet someone new. Ask them what their biggest achievement is, and then ask them to explain in detail how they accomplished it. If you're somewhat shy, this technique has the added advantage of being an instant ice breaker. Other people are usually glad to talk about themselves, and will be flattered that you think the details of what they did are worthwhile to know.

Every day, pay a little more attention to what works in the world around you. Over time you will see inspiration everywhere. That increases the inventory of examples that your mind can use to form ideas.

One of the most famous examples is Henry Ford: he got the idea for the moving assembly line for cars from the overhead rack of a slaughterhouse. The animal moves from station to station, while the workers stand still at each station. So Ford moved his cars on a rail through the factory to do the same thing.

Slaughterhouse

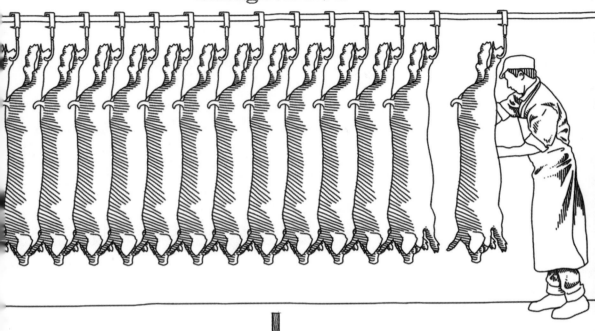

Ford Motor Co.

Presence of mind

You can also get better a the second step of the Art of Ideas: Presence of mind. This means you clear away your prior notions about the situation you face: what the problem is, what the solution is, what your goal is, what the question is, what the answer is, what you want, what you expect, what you like or dislike. You free your mind. That gives your brain the space and time to make its own connections. Presence of mind is difficult to foster, and it takes mental discipline to achieve. But it is crucial for creating good ideas—and it can make you happier and healthier too.

Here is what presence of mind looks like: Let's say two family members who are both very picky eaters are spending the night with you. You can't decide what to make for dinner that both will like. As you go up and down the aisles of the supermarket, the contents of your cart keep changing, but each time you look at the combination and know that your guests will not be happy with the dinner it will make.

Then you pass the egg case, and remember that both of your picky eaters love a big breakfast. "Breakfast" pops into your mind as a way to reach the wider goal of pleasing your guests.

So you switch your goal: you put back all the dinner ingredients and assemble breakfast instead. You take your guests out for dinner tonight and make them a big breakfast the following morning.

Presence of mind allowed you to let go of the original specific goal of making dinner for your guests. But it did not change your general goal completely: you kept the overall goal of trying to please your guests.

Go out to eat and make breakfast instead.

So how do you improve your presence of mind? It helps to realize you don't always need it. If you're working on a familiar task, go ahead and keep working until you finish, even if it takes until midnight. You already know what to do: you don't need a new idea, you don't need presence of mind. But if it's a task where you need a creative answer, don't work until midnight. Instead, carve out time for presence of mind and give your mind the space to wander.

In that case, when you need a new idea, throughout the workday try to take in as many examples from history as possible that might relate to your problem. Don't work late: spend the evening on something that gives your mind a rest. Go to the gym, have dinner with friends, or take a long shower, and above all get a good night's sleep. This greatly increases your chances of a flash of insight to solve your problem.

You can practice this discipline in smaller bits too, by scheduling time in your day for short walks, or making coffee, or some other activity where you give your mind a chance to clear, if only for fifteen minutes.

Another obstacle to presence of mind is distraction. Your mind flits from one activity to another. Some call it "multitasking," but in reality you cannot do many things at once. You do one thing in one moment, then something else in the next, and something else in the next. It's rapid sequential focus. But your brain needs time to shift from one thing to the other. So the faster and more often you shift, the worse you perform on each task. And there's not enough time between tasks for presence of mind.

The biggest enemy of presence of mind today is smart phones.

You might think that in a boring, useless meeting, there's no harm done by looking at your phone. But each time you look, you're eroding your presence of mind. It's much better just to sit there and let your mind wander, to give your brain a moment to relax in the midst of your hectic day. If your mind is on the phone, you'll miss the potential for a flash of insight. The irony is that the digital revolution makes examples from history easier to find, but it also makes presence of mind harder to achieve. As with excessive focus, reducing distraction is a matter of mental discipline. In theory, it's simple enough: just stop. Turn off your phone. But in practice, habits are hard to break, and more and more people expect you to reply within minutes to every message they send you. Start small and slowly, and build your tolerance for time away from your phone. As with any habit, it will take time and energy to break.

Flash of insight

It goes by many names:

A flash of insight.

The big "Aha!"

The Eurkea moment.

A spark of genius.

An epiphany.

It's the moment when a new idea forms in your head, and you suddenly see a way to accomplish something meaningful in your life. It's when examples from history come together with presence of mind to make a creative spark. This is not something you can trigger on demand. To improve your ability to generate ideas you must prepare for this moment as best you can. Improve your inventory of examples from history and curate your presence of mind. And then you wait.

A key part of presence of mind is to accept calmly that you might not have a flash of insight. That your search might lead nowhere. That maybe, just maybe, this particular problem is one that just can't be solved. In this case, go on with life, and turn to other problems. When the time is right, an idea will present itself. It could be in the shower or out for a run. Whenever it happens, you then need Resolution to act.

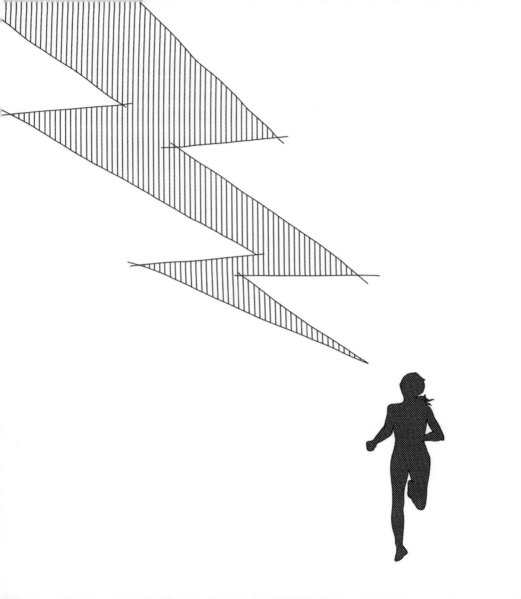

Resolution

Resolution is the crucial step when you set out to make your idea a reality. A flash of insight happens in an instant, but acting on it and implementing it can take days, months, or even years. The stronger your flash of insight, the stronger your resolution to see it through. You will have not just an idea but also a passion to make the idea come true.

Communicating your idea is often the first step in resolution. But here you face a dilemma: you may have to hide your passion at first. Unfortunately, many people think reason and passion are opposites. They are wary of ideas that seem to come from your heart, not from your head. Not everyone is like this, of course: they may be wise enough to understand that passion and reason can happily work together. But until you know that for sure, be careful. Be strategic. Think through how to do it, exactly.

Remember that you cannot expect other people to have presence of mind. They are not necessarily open to ideas that are different from their own. Give them the idea in pieces, just as it came together in your own mind, so that the pieces can come together in their minds too. That can help them see the idea. But that still doesn't mean they will like it.

For that, you need to tailor the message to your audience.

Do they like numbers? If so, mention numbers. Are they bureaucratic? If so, write up your idea in their standard forms or templates. Or they may always want to know what someone else thinks — so go to that other person first. You win people over one by one, according to how each one best takes in ideas.

In all cases, when you talk to someone about your idea, make sure that you do not ask them to judge it. Do not say, "What do you think of this idea?" or "Do you think this idea will work?" These kinds of questions invite them to criticize your idea. And that criticism will come as snap judgments—from examples they've seen in familiar situations. If your idea is a new one, it won't match their experience. So they'll tell you all the reasons your idea won't work.

Under the weight of relentless negativity, you'll give up on your idea before it's even off the ground.

So for your own sake, and for the sake of your idea, don't invite criticism. If you seek out criticism, you'll get it. Instead, seek first, understanding and second, suggestions for improvement. You and your idea will benefit far more.

1. **Explain your idea and how you got it.**

2. **Identify problems your idea will face when you put it into action.**

3. **Ask the person if they have ideas on how to solve those problems.**

4. **Ask if they have any other ideas to improve your idea.**

5. **Ask them to suggest anyone else you might ask these same questions.**

Actively seeking more ideas is a key aspect of resolution. Just because you've had a flash of insight doesn't mean that you no longer need examples from history and presence of mind. Remember how Gandhi took from Tolstoy after he took his big idea from Pankhurst? Many times, the original idea is not enough. Secondary flashes of insight shape the idea along the way. Resolution gives you the passion to take action on your idea, and part of that action should be to keep your mind open to other examples from history that your idea will need to succeed. Creativity is an ongoing cycle: first comes a flash of insight from examples from history and presence of mind, then resolution to act on the idea, then more examples and presence of mind give you another flash to adjust your idea, and then resolution again, on and on through the life of your idea.

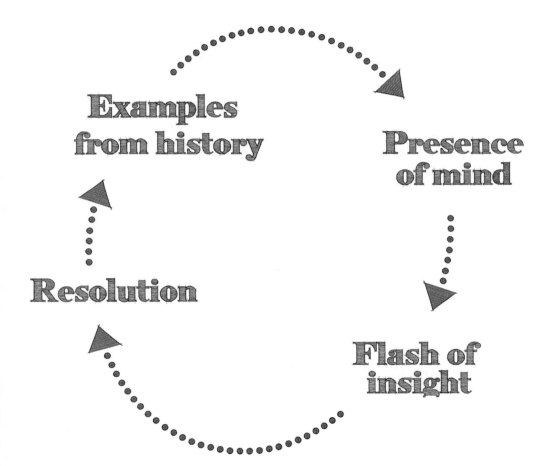

Personal strategy

Chapter 8

Now that you understand the four steps of creative thinking, we can ask: which step is hardest to do?

Let's take them one at a time.

Resolution (#4)

This means working hard on something you want, and seeing a way to achieve it. Do you know how to work hard? We bet you do. It's a matter of effort, pure and simple.

Your emotions can get in the way, of course. You can feel discouraged, lose confidence in your ability, or ignore further examples from history to improve your idea, but the mechanical steps of working hard are easy to figure out. You know how to do them.

Flash of insight (#3)

We saw that you cannot force this. It only happens when you have presence of mind and enough examples of the right kind stored in your memory. In that case, the flash of insight is easy – even effortless. It just happens.

But otherwise – without presence of mind or the right examples – the flash of insight is impossible. So it's either easy, or impossible. You can't learn how to do it better.

96

Examples from history (#1)

If you have the ability to read and understand this book, you have the ability to gather examples from history. It's a matter of finding stories of someone somewhere who succeeded at something, and studying how they did it. You know how to do that. We even gave you extra tips for this when using the insight matrix. Practice makes it easier to do each time.

Presence of mind (#2)

Ask yourself:

How good are you at clearing your mind of all your thoughts when facing a problem? Can you forget for just a while what your goals are, what you wish for, the question you're facing, all possible answers, and even the problem itself? Can you wipe your mind clean?

For most people, this is very, very hard to do.

But we're in luck. We have help in presence of mind. Over the past few years, various forms of meditation have become very popular for reducing stress to improve both mental and physical health. This is a very good trend. And there's another benefit: meditation helps presence of mind for creative thinking.

But not all types of meditation are equal in this.

The two most common types of meditation are:

Samatha

This is the original Hindu name for a method called 'focus' or 'monitoring' meditation in English. It clears your mind except for one single thing you focus on, such as your breathing, a point you stare at, or a part of your body. Mantra meditation is similar, in that it clears your mind of everything except the word you repeat as a mantra.

Vipassana

This is the original Hindu name for a method called 'insight' or 'acceptance' meditation in English. You let your thoughts wander freely without attachment to any of them. They just flow by. Even negative thoughts, like 'my boss hates me' or 'I hate my job', or happy thoughts too. You just move on to the next thought. You dwell on none of them.

We can see the difference between these two forms of clearing your mind. The first one empties it as much as possible, while the second one flushes it clean with a constant stream. Scientific research reports that both improve your health, but especially Vipassana. As you might guess, it's also harder to do. But we can see how Vipassana helps in creative thinking, by opening your mind to a multitude of thoughts, without barriers. That's why it's referred to as 'insight' meditation.

If we return to the examples of Picasso, Gandhi, Lake, and Hastings, we can see that a key part of their presence of mind was to let their minds wander in just this way. Each of them was doing one thing, and then something unexpected led them in a new and unforeseen direction. If instead they had focused solely on what they were doing, they would have never had their big flashes of insight.

We can also see from these examples that this 'free-thinking' aspect of presence of mind does not require the formal discipline of Vipassana. It's a state of mind you can carry with you wherever you go, whatever you do. Picasso, Gandhi, Lake, and Hastings were not meditating when their flashes of insight struck. But they did have presence of mind.

A key element of this day-to-day aspect of presence of mind is to accept the role of circumstance in the creative choices you face in life. It was not under Picasso's control whether Matisse existed. It was not under Gandhi's control that Emmeline Pankhurst existed. It was not under Reed Hastings's control that flat-membership gym fees existed. It was not under Lake's control that her sister became a fasion buyer who freely gave advice. If these things had not existed, they would not have had their big ideas.

Circumstance, not their own effort, provided the elements of their flashes of insight. Unfortunately, this view of circumstance contradicts a vast tradition of personal advice that has grown to universal appeal. It appears most forcefully in graduation speeches, both high school and college. On the next page are some samples broken out as **Positive Thinking** and the antidote, **Negative Thinking**.

No doubt: **Negative Thinking** of this kind is terrible. Sadly, many people grow up hearing this from family, friends, teachers, and often even themselves.

No doubt, **Positive Thinking** is better. But is it true?

From the point of view of the Art of Ideas, Positive Thinking lacks presence of mind.

It completely ignores the role of circumstance in what you can achieve. So we offer a third column, **Creative Thinking**.

Creative Thinking might not sound as motivating as **Positive Thinking**, but it's a better guide to living your life.

Picasso, Gandhi, Lake, Hastings and countless other success stories attest to this. And here's a big irony: if you ask any of those graduation speakers how exactly the succeeded themselves, you will find in most cases they did it through the steps of **Creative Thinking**.

Life is full of twists and turns far outside your control. Circumstance, not you, will determine what elements cross your path. Accepting that and noticing those elements you did not expect or even want, are key to the Art of Ideas.

And yet: there are also methods to increase your chance of finding circumstance in your favor.

And that's the subject of our next chapter.

Negative Thinking   # Positive Thinking

Negative Thinking		Positive Thinking
You're terrible at everything - don't even bother to try anything ambitious. You'll be disappointed.	or	You can achieve anything you want to if you believe in yourself, set clear goals, and work hard.
Don't do what you want -- you can't achieve it. Instead, listen to what others tell you to do.	or	Decide what you want most, set a clear long-term goal to get it, and work toward it step-by-step.
No matter how hard you work, you'll never achieve anything worthwhile. Don't even bother to try.	or	Where there's a will, there's a way.
If your plan doesn't reach your goal, it proves you're not worthy. Give up and try something easier instead.	or	If your plan does not reach your goal, keep your goal and change your plan.
If at first you don't succeed, it proves you're not worthy. Give up and try something easier instead.	or	If at first you don't succeed, try, try again.
Your own experience is worthless. Do what you're told. Don't even try to think for yourself.	or	Your own experience is the best source of ideas for what to do.
You're a fool to dream. Your life will never get better. You'll never get better. Accept it.	or	Never give up your dream.

Creative Thinking

or   You can do many things if you prepare
for opportunity, see it, and act on it.

or   You don't know what problem you can solve
until you see a way to solve it.

or   Where there's a way, there's a will.

or   If your plan does not reach your goal,
change either your goal or your plan.

or   If at first you don't succeed, study
why and consider changing your goal.

or   The experience of others is your
best source of ideas for what to do.

or   Adjust your dreams to circumstances.

Idea
Networking

Chapter 9

Networking used to be a formal affair. You join a club, like the Elks or Rotary or your college alumni association. The club holds events where you mingle with other club members and exchange business cards. The rules were clear: when a fellow club member calls for a favor, you do your best to help. And they do the same for you.

Globalization and information technology have blown up this model beyond recognition. Your network can now extend across the world, with hundreds or even thousands of people you've never met and never will. General networks like Facebook make it easy, and specialized networks like LinkedIn have tailored networking tools. The world is becoming one big network.

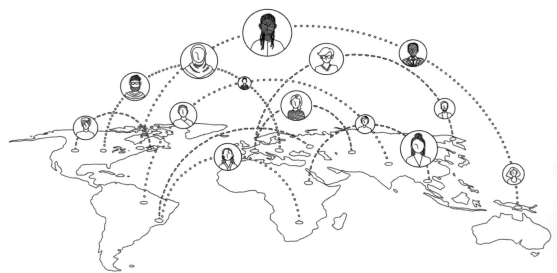

This global digital networking boom has turned face-to-face interaction of any kind into a networking event. Conventions, receptions, trade shows, even weddings and funerals, are all venues for adding people to your network. Everyone knows it, accepts it, and does it.

When you meet someone new, pull out your phones and exchange contact information. Your network has grown again.

But, this new world of networking all the time creates a big problem.

The old model of networking was a numbers game: get as many contacts as possible, because you never know which one might be useful in some unforeseen future situation. But now that someone's contacts can easily number in the thousands, you are just a drop in the bucket for them.

So now the problem is: how can you stand out in the crowd?

The solution to this problem is **Idea Networking**.

It's a way to seek not more and more contacts, but circumstances in your favor. It's a hunt for opportunity that you can't even know exists. It's a way to put you in situations that increase your chances for lightning to strike, where things fall into place, you see a way forward and the path is clear.

Idea Networking combines the best of the old club model of networking and the new global network explosion. The club had the advantage of a small group with one thing in common: the club itself. These two elements – small size, something in common – makes it much easier for the other person to connect with you and remember you.

The global digital network has the advantage of variety: you are not limited to just one club that came together for just one thing.
Idea Networking takes more thought and care than traditional networking in our digital age, but it's easier, more enjoyable, and far more productive. That thought and care is especially key at the start.

The first thing you need in Idea Networking is: an idea! And not just any idea.

You need: An idea

In the form of a question

That's truly interesting to you

And truly interesting to someone

Who has contacts in the field of your idea.

That is a very high standard. If you think of traditional networking, what is the content of what you say? What words do you actually speak? The typical advice is personal chit-chat. That is, get to know the new contact as a person. And if you're looking for a job, or at least thinking about it, you ask if the person knows of a job opening. Or if it's someone more senior, you ask advice.

Right away we can see that none of this is interesting to the other person. Even the personal chat seems like work, because the other person is not really looking to make new friends, so they don't really want to get to know you in any deep way. You're just a contact, the way they are just a contact for you. And time they spend getting to know you for real takes away time from meeting more contacts.

Traditional networking is a numbers game – the more the merrier. Idea Networking is not. It substitutes quality for quantity.

Once you develop your idea question, you need just one person to start with. If you don't know someone to ask, your question to your existing network can be, "Do you know someone in field X? I want to ask them a question."

When you find that person to ask, say briefly who you are – no more than ten words – and politely pose the question. You can do it by email or phone, but face-to-face is best. So have your question ready whenever you go to a gathering where you meet new people. Your question might need a few trials to make sure it's interesting enough to people in the field, and these casual meetings are a good place to do that.

Once you find someone to ask, and they answer, listen closely. After all, you are genuinely interested in the question. So their answer helps you learn. At the end, thank them. Then say this was so interesting, do they know anyone else you might ask? You might get ten names, you might get zero. Three is a good target.

So what do you do next?
The very same thing.

Ask those three people the same question. Or as you learn, your question might change. Three becomes nine becomes twenty-seven, and so on. By the time you get to twenty-six, you will know a lot about this field and have more than a dozen contacts of high quality in your field of interest.

We cite the number twenty-six because of our favorite example. A student from our Columbia MBA program graduated without a job, and the day after the graduation ceremony decided to use Idea Networking to find one. His name is Steven. He spoke some Portuguese and loved Brazil. He came up with a question in his field of interest – private equity, which is a branch of finance that invests in companies that are not listed on public stock exchanges.

Here was his question:

Is there private equity in Brazil?

Excellent. As an organized industry, private equity is quite new and does not yet exist in most countries. What about Brazil? Steven's question leads to many others:

How does it work in Brazil?

Are there local private equity companies?

Are they based in the political capital, Brasilia, or the commercial capital, Sao Paulo?

Is it local money or foreign investment?

And so on.

He then looked through the business cards he picked up at the many networking events his MBA program organized. He found one from an executive at a big international bank. That's where he started.

The twenty-sixth person got him a job in Brazil, doing private equity research for yet another big international bank. At no time did Steven ask for a job. By the time he got to twenty-six, he knew a lot about the field and was able to have a very sophisticated conversation. He was already a semi-expert. That twenty-sixth person happened to know someone down the hall looking for someone to fill a post in Brazil. In this way, Idea Networking cracks the oral network that fills most of the interesting jobs today.

And that's not the end of the story. When he got to Brazil, he found he was working for a terrible boss. Right away he started Idea Networking again. He had an even better question this time, because he was right there in Brazil. Nine months later, a Brazilian private equity firm offered him a job. He took it. So in two steps, he found the job of his dreams.

Most people who use Idea Networking report that they enjoy it far more than traditional networking. You learn more and more about something that interests you, and you meet new people who are interested in the same thing. Versus traditional networking, which feels like you're selling a product: yourself.

In Idea Networking you're not selling anything. You're learning.

We see that Idea Networking differs as well from the classic informational interview. Everyone knows that an informational interview is a step for seeking a job. That's not at all interesting to the person you talk to. But you can even turn an informational interview into Idea Networking: try to judge what the person you're talking to finds interesting, and then ask an interesting question. The three contacts you get from that do not have to be from that company. It's even better if they are not. You are exploring a field, not a company. A field is so much wider, with so many more possible circumstances that might turn out in your favor.

Conclusion

Now that you know how creative ideas really work, we leave you with one last thought:

the Art of Ideas is also a science.

When Einstein's theory of relativity came out in 1905, many physicists accused him of plagiarism. Five other scientists, from five different countries, had already proposed the five parts of his theory:

Maxwell – light as both energy and mass	**Scotland**
Poincaré – relativity of time	**France**
Lorentz – constant speed of light	**Holland**
Minkowski – space-time equations	**Lithuania**
Mach – mass tied to speed	**Austria**

We recognize now that Einstein's new theory was not plagiarism, but creative combination. Otherwise known as the Art of Ideas. This is not a criticism – it was a great achievement for Einstein to search through the myriad advances in physics at the time, by hundreds of scientists, and select just the right elements to make his new combination.

In his famous book, The Structure of Scientific Revolutions, Thomas Kuhn makes a key distinction between 'normal' science and 'revolutionary' science. Normal science repeats variations of previous ideas and results. Revolutionary science creates new ideas, with new results. And it happens through creative combination. His own study of the subject began with Copernicus, who replaced the idea of the earth as the center of the universe with the sun at the center of the solar system, with the earth one of several planets in orbit around it. This breakthrough launched the Scientific Revolution.

How did Copernicus do it? He combined three previous elements:

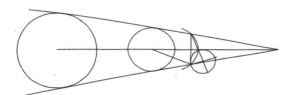

First, the Greek astronomer Aristarchus of Samos proposed the sun as the center of the solar system. That was more than seventeen centuries before Copernicus. It was a well-known theory in the field.

Second, over those seventeen centuries astronomers continued to measure the movements of heavenly bodies – all before the telescope. Copernicus had their results at hand.

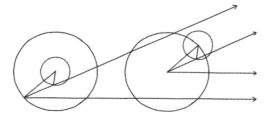

Third, recent advances in trigonometry made it possible for Copernicus to calculate arcs, speeds and times from that wealth of data from previous astronomers.

Kuhn concludes:

"The cosmological frame in which his astronomy was embedded, his physics, terrestrial and celestial, and even the mathematical devices that he employed to make his system give adequate predictions, are all in the tradition established by ancient and medieval scientists." [1]

1) Kuhn page 181

In other words:
The elements were not new.
The combination was new.
Which now we recognize as –

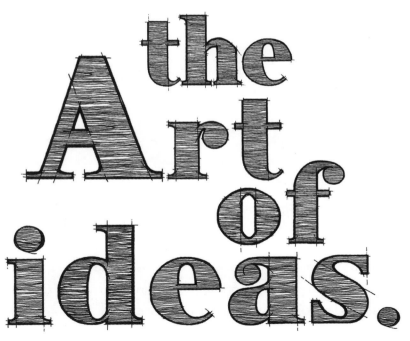

the Art of ideas.

For Kuhn's 'normal' science, you don't need the Art of Ideas. For new ideas in science, you do – just like any other field. Isaac Newton, the founder of modern physics, said as much in his famous quote,

If I have seen farther, it is by standing on the shoulders of giants.

Newton names all the previous scientists he 'stole' from for his own work. But he doesn't tell us – he also stole the quote:

Bernard of Chartres: "We are like dwarfs on the shoulders of giants..."

Isaac Newton: "If I have seen farther, it is by standing on the shoulders of giants."

Look at the speeches of Nobel Prize winners in science. They're all online. The footnotes are just as long as the speech. The winners recognize how much they stand on the shoulders of those who came before them. And so should we.

Art or science – creative combination is the secret of success for new ideas in any field. And now you too know the secret. You are ready to become, in your own way, in your own time, in your own field of interest–

an Artist of Ideas.

About us

Amy Murphy -- Author, Book Designer

Amy is a licensed architect in the state of New York. She advises business clients on innovation, strategy and creativity with PwC's Strategy& as a Director with PwC US. Amy teaches at Columbia Business School Executive Education, holds a MBA from Columbia Business School and a Bachelor of Architecture from Cornell University.

Laura Dabalsa -- Illustrator

Laura is a Visual Arts major at Columbia University specializing in painting, sculpture, illustration and new media art. Laura complements coursework in the arts with studies in social science, language and coding, as well as serving as an active leader and graphic designer for several Columbia student groups.

William Duggan -- Author

William Duggan is on the faculty of Columbia Business School, where he teaches the art of ideas to MBA and Executive MBA students and executives from around the world. He worked many years as a strategy advisor and consultant, and has BA, MA and PhD degrees from Columbia University.